Hangin' With
O-TOWN

by Michael-Anne Johns

SCHOLASTIC INC.

New York   Toronto   London   Auckland   Sydney
Mexico City   New Delhi   Hong Kong   Buenos Aires

TOWN

Front Cover: Eddie Mallun; Back Cover: Anthony Cutajar; Page 3: Joseph Galea; Page 4: Joseph Galea; Page 5: (top) Ron Davis/Shooting Star; (bottom) James Patrick Cooper/Retna Ltd.; Pages 6-9: Joseph Galea; Pages 13-15: Joseph Galea; Page 16: Ron Davis/Shooting Star; Pages 17-19: Joseph Galea; Page 20: Ron Davis/Shooting Star; Page 21-23: Joseph Galea; Pages 24-25: South Beach Photo Agency; Page 26: Tara Canova/Retna Ltd.; Page 27: Joseph Galea; Page 28: (left) South Beach Photo Agency; (right) Joseph Galea; Page 29: Joseph Galea; Page 30: Ron Davis/Shooting Star; Page 31: Joseph Galea: Page 32: (left) South Beach Photo Agency; (right) Tara Canova/ Retna Ltd.; Page 33: Joseph Galea; Page 35: Joseph Galea; Page 36: (top right) South Beach Photo Agency; (bottom) Joseph Galea; Page 37: Joseph Galea; Pages 44-48: Joseph Galea.

ISBN 0-439-32696-6

Book design by Keirsten Geise

12 11 10 9 8 7 6 5 4 3 2 1   1 2 3 4 5 6/0

Printed in the U.S.A.
First Scholastic printing, November 2001

CONTENTS

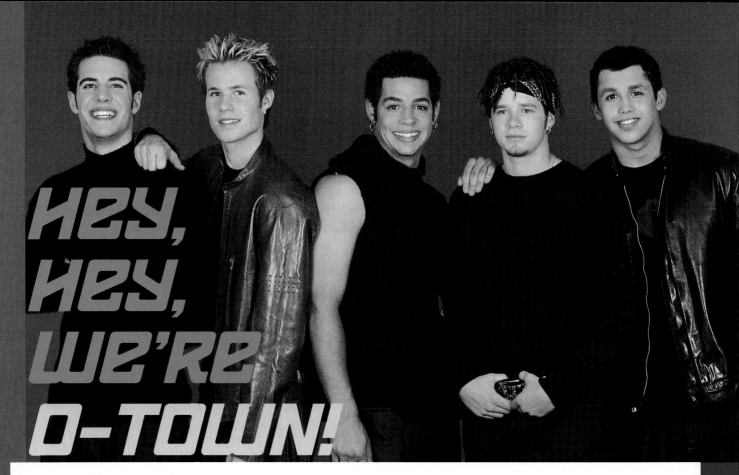

HEY, HEY, WE'RE O-TOWN!

Come on in! O-Town is in the house and ready to meet and greet all their fans. You're invited to spend some time with Ashley, Jacob, Erik, Dan, and Trevor. See how these outrageous hotties fill 24/7.

You'll see them from a fans'-eye view in concert and at play. You'll get to know them up close and really personal. Dig into special head-to-toe lists of their facts and faves! Did you know Ashley confessed that he has been known to sneak into the closet to chow down on candy? Or that Erik admits you might not want to see O-Town when they rehearse for a show: "We don't do our hair when we go to rehearsal — we look really gross!" Or that Jacob's favorite nail polish color is black — true! Or that Dan could live indefinitely on McDonald's Chicken McNuggets and fries? Or that Trevor never goes into the studio without a supply of Mint Milano cookies?

In *Hangin' With O-Town* you'll get an insiders look at the O-Town boys, plus crazy cool photos and pinups of them. Don't waste a minute more . . . read on!

The original eight boys hoping to make the cut on *Making the Band*: Top (l. to r.), Paul Martin, Erik-Michael Estrada, Ashley Parker Angel, Ikaika Kahoano; Bottom (l. to r.), Bryan Chan, Jacob Underwood, Mike Miller, and Trevor Penick.

O-Town . . . heads together!

The video shoot was full of splishing and splashing — and a few spills.

When Ashley, Dan, Jacob, Erik, and Trevor strode onto the set of their first video shoot, they were excited and a little bit nervous. But soon things began to loosen up as they dove headfirst into the singing and dancing.

"I took the first spill — a mild spill," laughs Dan. "I slipped and I caught myself. Erik took a full-out underwater scuba dive spill. I exaggerate, but he took a large jump and hit the floor real hefty. But I'm not going to lie — I hit the floor, too. We all knew it was going to happen at some point during the day; we were taking bets on who was going to do it first, and that was me."

Elizabeth Hurley, J.Lo, Cameron Diaz, Charlize Theron, Jennifer Love Hewitt, Janet Jackson, Carmen Electra, Amy Smart, and Madonna — they are all mentioned in the group's first single. Trevor says the one he would definitely like to meet is Madonna. Why? "She's MADONNA and she's been around for so long," he explains. "I want to hear what she thinks about it, from someone who is respected and has been in the industry so long."

"I almost took a digger once," recalls Ashley. "We do kind of like a moonwalk backslide and it is just so slippery that I lost my footing, but I caught myself before I fell. I was conscious of it, but you kind of have to forget about that because you have to dance. You can't be too careful or otherwise it looks funny."

Jacob gets miked up so we can hear his glorious voice in the video!

Ashley is a true star! Here, he takes a break from shooting.

Dan gets some last-minute suggestions from director Dave Meyers.

O-Town's Fun & Games

Being one of the top pop bands is hard work, but you know the saying, "All work and no play . . ." Check out Dan, Erik, Trevor, Ashley, and Jacob as they take some time out for a few laughs.

Getting ready for takeoff!

Erik and Ashley — O-Town's flyboys!

O 11

Ashley has hoop dreams.

And Erik wins the game — and has a new buddy to take home!

After an impromptu performance while O-Town was staying at the famed Atlantis hotel in the Bahamas, they chatted with fans and friends.

The boys were all business when it came to picking the winner of the "Making the Fan" Contest. At their fave NYC hangout, Planet Hollywood, the guys picked sixteen-year-old Angel Zaccaro.

The O-Town boys just goofing around!

When O-Town made an in-store appearance at the NYC record store Coconuts, the fans made the group so happy that they gave them a gift — a mini-concert!

ASHLEY — HE'S THE ANGEL

Blue-eyed, blond-haired babe Ashley Parker Angel first showed musical talent when his piano teacher mom, Paula, taught him how to play when he was only four years old. His stepdad, Ron, schooled a thirteen-year-old Ashley on how to play the guitar. But it was Ashley who added that golden touch to his musical repertoire — his voice. He started singing just after he began talking.

After high school, Ashley enrolled in college and performed at local clubs and events. He mostly sang his own original songs, and a radio station was ready to send him into the studio to record one of his tunes. Shortly after that, Ashley saw an interesting notice at an acting class he was taking — it was a call for auditions for Lou Pearlman, the mastermind behind 'N Sync and the Backstreet Boys. Pearlman was putting together a "boy band" and was holding auditions all over the country. That was all Ashley needed to hear. . . . He was on his way to Las Vegas for what he hoped would be his big break.

Ashley brings a major sense of humor to the group, and he knows a whole lot about music, too.

Ashley:

From Head to Toe

Name: Ashley Parker Angel
Nickname: Ash
Birthdate: August 1, 1981
Astro Sign: Leo
Birthplace: Reddings, CA (near Sacramento)
Parents: Mom, Paula; Stepdad, Ron
Siblings: Brother, Taylor; Two half sisters, Annie and Emily
Pet: Dog named Chang
Height: 6 feet
Hair: Blond
Eyes: Blue
Instruments He Plays: Guitar and piano
College: Shasta College

Piercings: One in his left ear
Making the Band **Audition Location:** Las Vegas, NV
O-Town Personality: "The funny one" and "the leader"
Best Traits: "Loving, patient, honest, dedicated, focused, comical, charismatic, charming, and everybody's best friend."
Worst Traits: "Maybe [I'm] a little vain sometimes. Too focused or 'into' what I'm concentrating on so that I have trouble deciphering the outside world."
Most Important Person: "My mom — she's my hero."
Future Goal: To be an actor
Best Friend: His cousin Casey
Early Jobs: Worked at the ShopGo in his hometown, and as a lifeguard
Hobbies: Writing screenplays, watching movies
Sports He Likes: Scuba diving, snowboarding, racquetball, tennis, basketball
First Concert Attended: Third Eye Blind
O-Town Voice: Tenor
Superhero Persona: Superman

Faves

Food: Lasagna
Cereal: Sugar Smacks
Coffee: Starbucks
Drink: Fruit smoothies
Sport: Basketball
Movies: *The Matrix*, *Star Wars*

TV Shows: *Friends*, *Seinfeld*, *The Simpsons*, and MTV
***Friends*' Character:** Rachel
Comic Book Character: Superman
Comedians: Robin Williams, Whoopi Goldberg, Billy Crystal
Singer: Michael Jackson
Cologne: Aqua deGio, Perry Ellis
Boxers or Briefs: Calvin Klein briefs (according to Trevor, Ashley wears "tighty-whiteys")
Sheets: His *Star Wars* ones — he brought them to Orlando with him
Possession: His journal and his laptop computer
Place: St. Thomas, Virgin Islands
Amusement Park: Universal's Islands of Adventure — his fave ride is Spider-Man, and his fave roller coaster is Dueling Dragons.

3 Wishes

1 "(For) my family to be taken care of the way I feel they should."

2 "Success in life."

3 "More wishes!"

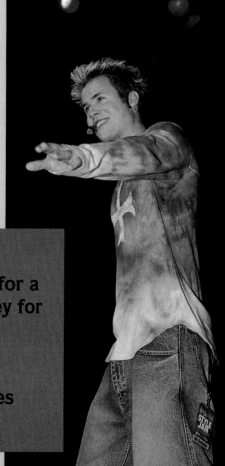

Little-Known Facts:

- Ashley actively supported and attended rallies for a legislative bill in California to raise more money for school libraries and classrooms.
- Ashley is the voice of "Alex" on the Sony Playstation game, LUNAR.
- When Ashley was six years old, his fave jammies were a Superman suit with a red cape.

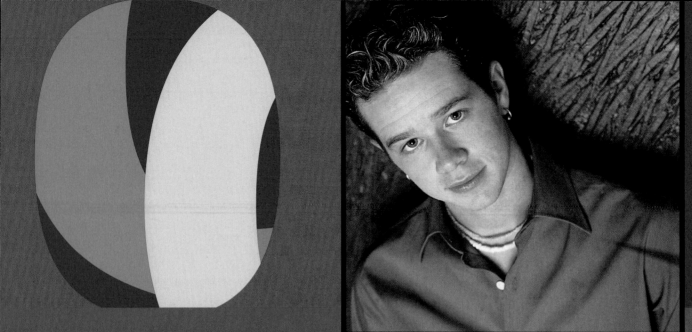

JUST JACOB

Education is very important to Jacob's family. He has 37 cousins, all of whom have gone to college. Jacob planned on going, too, although he always knew he wanted to concentrate on music. Even before college was a glimmer, Jacob started taking voice lessons in the seventh grade and began playing the guitar and other instruments even earlier.

Jacob heard about the *Making the Band* audition from a friend who had checked it out on the Internet. He was ready to sign up, but he knew that if he succeeded he would forgo his college education — for a while, at least. It was a major decision — and not an easy one. But when his family gave Jacob their blessing, he headed to the Hard Rock Café in Los Angeles to audition for the TV series *Making the Band*.

The audition was a dream come true for Jacob. "I always wanted the opportunity to sing and show my talents in front of someone in the music industry that could make a difference and honestly tell me if I had what it takes or not," Jacob says of his tryout. "It was the opportunity."

"I think music is the highest form of expression, and I love the idea of expressing my thoughts and feelings to such a wide audience through music," Jacob says.

Jacob
Stax of facts

Name: Jacob Christopher Underwood
Birthdate: April 25, 1980
Astro Sign: Taurus
Birthplace: El Cajon, CA (near San Diego)
Parents: Mother, Mechele
Siblings: Brother, Brian; sister, Danielle
Height: 5 feet 10 ½ inches
Hair: Dirty blond (naturally) — now dark brown or red and in dreadlocks
Eyes: Blue
Instruments He Plays: Guitar, saxophone, piano, clarinet, bass, violin
High School: Valhalla High School
Piercings: Both ears
Tattoos: One on his lower back
***Making the Band* Audition Location:** Los Angeles, CA
O-Town Personality: "Driven — a perfectionist"
Best Traits: "A funny guy who keeps things going. I'm constantly reinventing myself."
Worst Traits: "I guess because I'm always changing, I never let anyone — except for a few friends — know who I really am."
Early Job: Worked at a golf course in San Diego
Sports He Likes: Water polo, wrestling, baseball, soccer, basketball, surfing, skating
O-Town Voice: Tenor
Superhero Persona: Batman with a little bit of Spider-Man

THE MANY LOOKS OF JACOB

Faves

Food: Spinach
Cereal: Honey Snacks, Golden Grahams, Apple Jacks — "anything with high levels of sucrose or fructose."
Movie: *Me, Myself, and Irene*
Singer: Michael Jackson
Childhood Memory: "Christmas — all my family gathers at my Grandpa's and he dresses up like Santa Claus."
Nail Polish Color: Black
Cologne: Clinique Happy for Men
Boxers or Briefs: Boxer briefs
Charities: Christian Youth Theater and Christian Community Theater — "I grew up in it and it is a very good organization."
Alternative Band: Papa Roach
Pastime: Playing his guitar
Sport: Skateboarding

It's a family affair! Jacob was really glad his sister Danielle (above) and his brother Brian (below) could join the O-Town crew down in the Bahamas for the "Making the Fan" contest festivities.

Little-Known Facts:

- Jacob is one of 38 cousins.
- He used to dye his hair a different color every month.
- If Jacob were stranded on a deserted island, he'd bring his guitar, Bible, and writing book.

The group's second video, for "All or Nothing," hung tight in the number one spot on MTV's *Total Request Live.* Go O-Town!

DAN THE MAN

Though Dan was the last to join O-Town — he got the call from music mentor Lou Pearlman when Ikaika Kahoano dropped out in the middle of the first season of *Making the Band* — he is hardly the low man in the group. Dan had made it through the first cut to the twenty-five guys originally brought to Orlando, but he didn't make the cut at eight. However, Trevor, Ashley, Jacob, and Erik all say that he was their first choice to replace Ikaika.

The eldest of four children, Dan had gone back to Ohio after he wasn't asked to join the O-Town house. He returned to the University of Cincinnati where he was studying music. As a matter of fact, Dan was studying for exams when he received the call to fly down to Orlando for a second shot at joining the group.

It wasn't an easy transition since the other guys had already spent weeks working with choreographers, producers, and voice coaches. But Dan dove in. "I was immediately embraced as a performer," he recalls, "but it took a long time to get bonded with the guys. That was the tough part." Now all five are the best of friends!

Dan *The Basics*

Name: Dan Mark Miller
Birthdate: September 4, 1980
Astro Sign: Virgo
Birthplace: Lanconia, New Hampshire
Family Home: Twinsburg, Ohio (near Cleveland)
Parents: Mom, Angela; Dad, Mark
Siblings: Sister, Allyson; brothers Kevin and Adam
Height: 6 feet
Hair: Brown
Eyes: Blue
College: University of Cincinnati College Conservatory of Music

3 Wishes

1 To be able to follow his dreams.

2 To meet Michael Jackson.

3 That people would respect one another.

"People can say whatever they want," insists Dan when asked about some critics saying that O-Town is a put-together group. "We know our situation is strange because we didn't have to go through the struggles that a lot of other groups went through, but that's why this is our story."

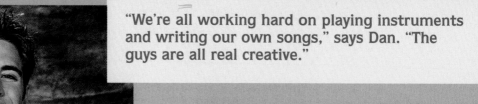

"We're all working hard on playing instruments and writing our own songs," says Dan. "The guys are all real creative."

Hobbies: Hang out with friends, play cards, shoot pool, go to the mall
First Concert Attended: Marky Mark and the Funky Bunch
O-Town Voice: Baritone/tenor
Superhero Persona: Mighty Mouse

***Making the Band* Audition Location:** Nashville, TN
O-Town Personality: "Humble, quiet, and outgoing."
Best Traits: He's not afraid to share.
Worst Traits: "Sometimes I let things go because I don't like to be mean and hurt feelings. Sometimes you need to be a little on the meaner side to make a change. I can't do that."
Early Job: A cook in a restaurant
Childhood Ambition: To be an architect or an Olympic diver

Faves

Fast Food: McDonald's Chicken McNuggets and fries
Cereal: Rice Krispies Treats
TV Show: MTV's *Real World* (Hawaii)
Music: R&B
R&B Musicians: Stevie Wonder, Jodeci, Eric Benet
Pop Singers: Michael Jackson, Janet Jackson
Possession on the Road: His CD player
Article of Clothing to Buy: Shoes
Clothing Style: Urban — T-shirt, jeans, and hat or bandana
Sports He Likes: Basketball (he played varsity all four years in high school), pool
Sports Team: Cleveland Indians
Cologne: Tommy
Childhood Memory: When he was in third grade and played a tree in a school play
Place: California
Boxers or Briefs: Boxer briefs

Little-Known Facts:

- Dan is more of a stay-at-home kinda guy than the others in O-Town. "I'm not too much of a partier."
- The qualities Dan looks for in a girl are "the best personality possible, outgoing, energetic, and physically attractive."
- Dan was All-Conference when he played high school basketball.

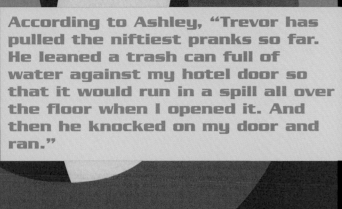

According to Ashley, "Trevor has pulled the niftiest pranks so far. He leaned a trash can full of water against my hotel door so that it would run in a spill all over the floor when I opened it. And then he knocked on my door and ran."

Trevor — He's Terrific

This California cutie was truly meant to be part of a boy band! One of Trevor's most memorable experiences was attending a Backstreet Boys concert where he sat in the third row — he even reached out and touched A.J. McLean's hand!

Well, perhaps that touch sparked something in Trevor, because even when he was attending college at California State at Fullerton, he wasn't embarrassed to admit he was a fan of the teenybopper band the Backstreet Boys. As a matter of fact, Trevor admits his college fraternity brothers used to tease him about his BSB devotion. But that didn't bother Trevor because, he admits, "I've always wanted to entertain. I've always been a big performer."

So when Trevor heard about the *Making the Band* auditions, he jumped at the chance. "It seemed like the perfect opportunity," Trevor says. "It was right up my alley."

So right that Trevor Penick was picked as one of the final five!

Trevor is one of the O-Town five now, but it was a close call. "I made my audition tape with a friend of mine, but only he was given a callback," recalls Trevor. "I went with him anyway, because he's my best friend, but I never imagined they would pick me!"

Trevor: Totally

Name: Trevor Lee Scott Penick
Nickname: Midol — his college frat brothers gave it to him because he could be moody
Birthdate: November 16, 1979
Astro Sign: Scorpio
Birthplace: Rancho Cucamonga, CA
Parents: Mother, Doris; Father, Clifton
Siblings: Sisters Traci, Rani, and Vanessa
Pet: Dog named Lucy after comedienne Lucille Ball
Height: 6 feet 1 inch
Hair: Brown
Eyes: Brown
College: California State at Fullerton (Theater major)
Fraternity: Pi Kappa Phi (Trevor is member #269 — he signs it on his autographs)
Piercings: Both ears
Making the Band Audition Location: Los Angeles, CA
Best Traits: "Thoughtful, caring, outgoing, and funny"

Worst Traits: "[I'm] irresponsible sometimes and a little dirty when it comes to papers around my room."
Most Important Person: His dad
Best Friend: Jerrod Kilde
Early Job: He worked at Quakes Stadium.
Hobbies: Hanging out at the beach
First Concert Attended: Boyz II Men
Celebrity Crushes: Britney Spears and Alyssa Milano
O-Town Voice: Bass/baritone
Superhero Persona: Batman

Faves

Cereal: Cinnamon Toast Crunch
Cookies: Mint Milano
Sports: Golf, basketball
Music: Rap, R&B, country, pop, and alternative
TV Shows: *Saved by the Bell*, *Fresh Prince of Bel Air*, MTV's *TRL*
Actor: Will Smith
Will Smith Movie: *Enemy of the State*
Singer: Will Smith
Will Smith Song: "Who Am I?"
O-Town Song: "The Painter"
Actor: Denzel Washington

Number: 5 — "It was my favorite number all through high school. I had four friends that hung out together — just friends, and we called ourselves Five."

Colognes: Versaci Dreamer, Chrome

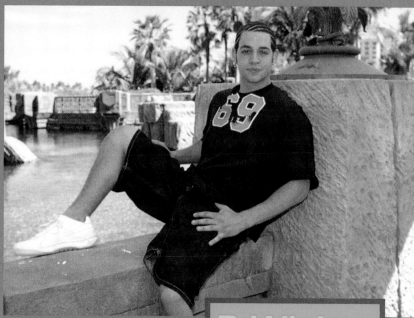

Boxers or Briefs: Boxer briefs
Possessions: Family pictures — he always brings them on the road with him
Place: Toronto, Canada

Little-Known Facts:

- Trevor has a Backstreet Boys T-shirt on his bedroom wall.
- Trevor was senior class president of his high school class.
- Trevor's first kiss was when he was twelve years old and in the eighth grade.
- Trevor is afraid of spiders.

3 Wishes

1 My parents will see me live a full life.
2 To have fame.
3 To be a good person.

Extraordinary Erik

Erik's voice has been magic ever since he was a little boy. "I started singing in church around the age of seven," the New York City boy recalls. "People would come up to me crying and hugging me and saying my voice touched them."

At Erik's house music was always playing, and Erik loved to sing along with the radio, TV, and records. Yet no one ever thought Erik was going to make music his career — no one but Erik.

When he was still in high school, Erik's family moved from New York to Melbourne, Florida. After high school, Erik was performing at local events and looking for a way to break into the biz. It came when he happened to stop by his parents' house and the TV was on. "I saw the announcement for [the *Making the Band* auditions] on E! Entertainment TV," Erik recalls. "I don't even watch TV, and I happened to see it twice in one day. I had a gut feeling about it — I had to do it." The rest, as they say, is history!

Bet you didn't know that Erik and Ashley had a bit of disagreement over how they sign their autographs. "I put 'Love' on all my autographs and he never did," explains Erik.

"I've written 'Love' since the eighth grade!" Ashley shot back. You'll have to get their autographs to see how they resolved it.

Essential Erik

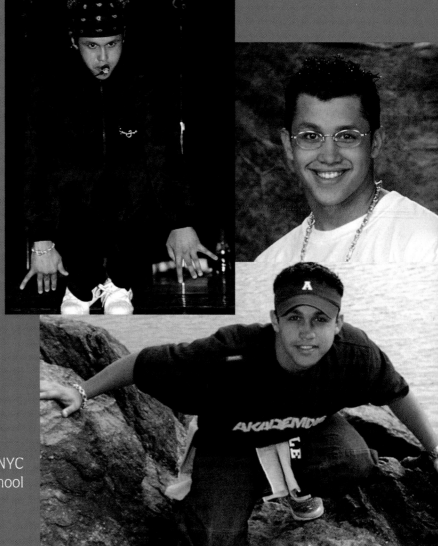

Name: Erik-Michael Estrada

Nickname: Logan (It's after the comic book character the Flash, whose real name is Logan.)

Birthdate: September 23, 1979

Astro Sign: Libra

Birthplace: Bronx, NY

Current Residence: Palm Bay, FL

Parents: Mom, Miky; Stepdad, Mel

Siblings: none

Height: 6 feet 1 inch

Hair: Dark brown

Eyes: Blue

High Schools: Mount Saint Michael in NYC and graduated from Melbourne High School after his family moved to Florida

Making the Band Audition Location: Orlando, FL

O-Town Personality: "[Being] crazy, and a leader are the strongest, but being a listener is an essential part of [being in a] group."

Best Traits: "I love to learn — I'm a sponge."

Worst Traits: "I'm a dreamer and I play too many practical jokes on people."

Most Important Person: His grandmother

Hobbies: Driving his car, writing songs

First Concert Attended: Carmen — a contemporary Christian artist

O-Town Voice: Tenor

Superhero Persona: Wolverine

Faves

Meal: His mom's vegetable lasagna

Cereal: Golden Crisps and Golden Grahams

Sport: Handball

Actor: Al Pacino

Actress: Michelle Pfeiffer

TV Channels: E! channel, Comedy Central, MTV

Cartoons: *The Simpsons, Thundercats, Duck Tales*

Reading Material: Comic books
Book: *Animal Farm* by George Orwell
Musicians: Boyz II Men, Mariah Carey, and Michael Jackson
O-Town Song: "One Heart"
Cologne: Polo Sport
Boxers or Briefs: Boxer briefs
Pastimes: Going shopping in New York City and then grabbing a slice of pizza
Possession: His cell phone — "I'm too much of a social person and I need to talk to my mom."
Theme Park: Disney World — especially Downtown Disney
Theme Park Ride: Disney World's Tower of Terror
School Subjects: Chorus, English literature, and humanities
Way to Relax: Go on his JetSki

3 Wishes

1 "(That) my parents' health would remain great and (they will) live a full life."
2 "To perform onstage and bring forth beautiful music for people's enjoyment."
3 "Throw all the thoughts of war out of the heads of everyone."

Little-Known Facts:

- According to Trevor, Ashley, Dan, and Jacob, Erik is the messiest of the five!
- Erik says the book that influenced him the most was *The Celestine Prophecy*.
- If Erik could have superpowers, they would be "advanced healing power like Wolverine and I would be able to run really fast like the Flash."

Backstage Pass to
O-Town in Concert

O-Town's in the house! Get up close and personal as Ashley, Jacob, Dan, Trevor, and Erik bring the audience to their feet at this Cleveland, Ohio, concert. As the old saying goes . . . Cleveland Rocks! Especially when O-Town is there.

For Erik, Jacob, Dan Trevor, and Ashley, the music is the most important thing...

In Concert

They put
their hearts
and souls
into their
performance...

In Concert

And it's just
for their fans
— that's YOU!

O-Town Rap Session

When Ashley, Trevor, Erik, Dan, and Jacob get together, you never know what's gonna be said! Check out these Q&A's — O-Town style.

Erik

Q: How was it to live your life for the last two years in front of cameras for *Making the Band?*

Jacob: "In the very beginning the cameras were very difficult to deal with, but after a couple of weeks it just became regular. We didn't realize that they were there. [At first] it was very uncomfortable."

Q: What do you think of the WB series *Popstars?*

Trevor: "I think all across the board we're pretty excited to see how that's going to turn out, just because we've all been through it," he told a newspaper reporter when the girls' version of *Making the Band* first appeared on the WB. "It's going to be weird to see it from the other side."

O-Town's ready for a question-session!

Trevor

Q: What do you tease one another about?

Jacob: "Ashley's [like] the girl of the group. He has to do his own hair, even if someone already did it. He'll be like, 'Cool, perfect, thanks,' and five minutes later he's in the bathroom fixing it. At photo shoots, he checks out his [butt] in the mirror to make sure his pants fit right. We call him Vanilla Ice because he bites down to make his jawbone look stronger in pictures. Erik used to do the 'I'm a model' look, too, but we gave him so much [grief] he stopped!"

Ashley: "Trevor is Extreme Man. If he's sad, he wants to cry, and if he's angry, he's irate. There's no middle ground. Dan's the responsible one. He takes care of the bills and cleans without anyone asking him to."

Ashley

Jacob

Q: Do you guys ever fight?

Ashley: "There is no way you can have a group like this, and spend so much time together, without having individual bickering. For the most part, honestly, we are very lucky that this entire situation hasn't affected our friendship. We are very tight and we became each other's family. We are like brothers, but, yes, we do have arguments."

Trevor: "We work it out."

Ashley: "We communicate and that is one of the things Boyz II Men told us — just make sure that we communicate."

Dan: "We're like brothers, but brothers argue, too. We fight over the stupidest things that basically don't need to be fought over and are forgotten immediately."

Dan

So long for now!

Q: Were you always yourselves when in front of the camera?

Erik: "As real as you can be when you're having a camera follow you 24/7. It wasn't like we were holding back because we were afraid. Most of it was we weren't saying [things] because we didn't know each other. I wasn't going to offend somebody I just met three months [before] and who I'm possibly going to be in a band with."

47

"I know a joke!" tried the rabbit. "It's going to make you laugh!"

"NO!" bristled the bear.

"I'M GOING TO BITE YOU IN HALF."

MORE BEAR JOKES

Q: Why do bears have fur coats?
A: Because they'd look very silly in Anoraks

HA! HA!

"But I'm tiny," the rabbit babbled.
"I'll be gone in one munch!

Wouldn't you maybe... rather... have a really BIG lunch?"

"END OF STORY!"
snarled the bear.
"I don't want your maybes!
What do you think this is...

A BEDTIME BOOK FOR BABIES?"

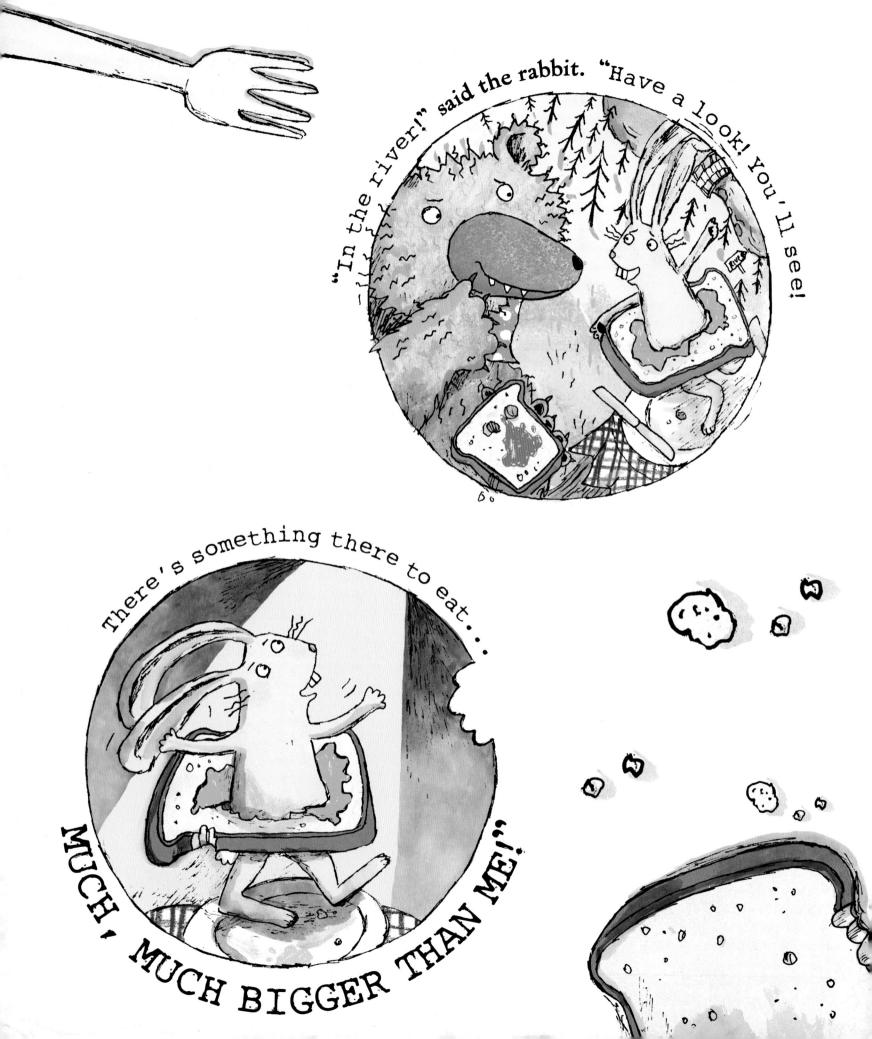

"Much, much bigger?" muttered the bear.

"Hmmmmmm…"

He kept a tight hold on the rabbit but he walked back through the woods and… took a little look in the river.

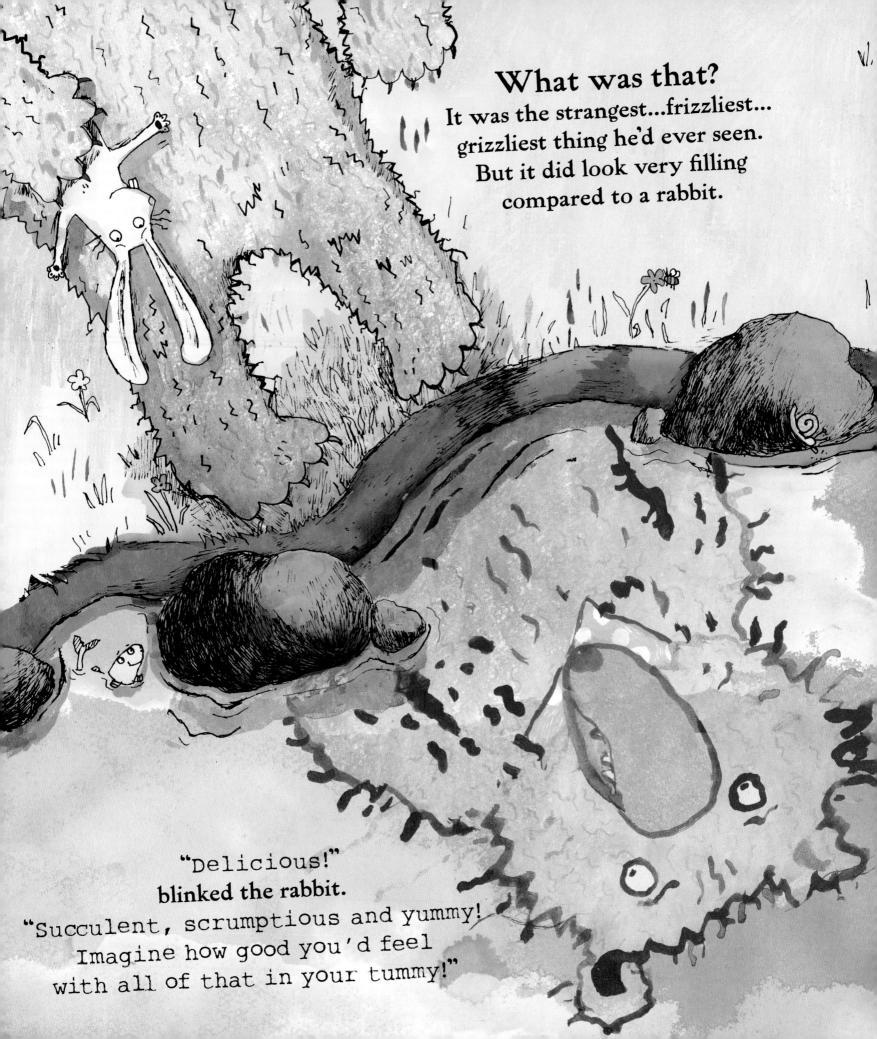

What was that?
It was the strangest...frizzliest...
grizzliest thing he'd ever seen.
But it did look very filling
compared to a rabbit.

"Delicious!"
blinked the rabbit.
"Succulent, scrumptious and yummy!
Imagine how good you'd feel
with all of that in your tummy!"

The Grizzly Bear with the Frizzly Hair
dropped the rabbit and
he grabbed at the thing in the river.
But it grabbed straight back.

He bared his teeth.
But it bared its teeth back.

"Oh dear!" sighed the rabbit. "I'll tell you what I think. It reckons you are just some...

GREAT BIG GOOFY WIMP!"

The Grizzly Bear with Frizzly Hair swiped a giant paw at the thing in the river.

But the thing in the river swiped a giant paw back.

That was too much.

In a rage, the bear jumped
at his own reflection.

And he sank deep down
into the water.

Deep...

down...

into...

the water.

The rabbit didn't hang about. He went skittling off as fast as he could.

"COME BACK!" gurgled the bear, wrinkling his soggy nose.

"I hope you enjoyed the story," called the rabbit, "BECAUSE THIS IS AS FAR AS IT GOES!"

RABBIT LAND welcome

And with that he was gone, safely into the long grass,

checking his toes,
checking his knees,
checking his tummy, his chest and his head.

And they were all still there!

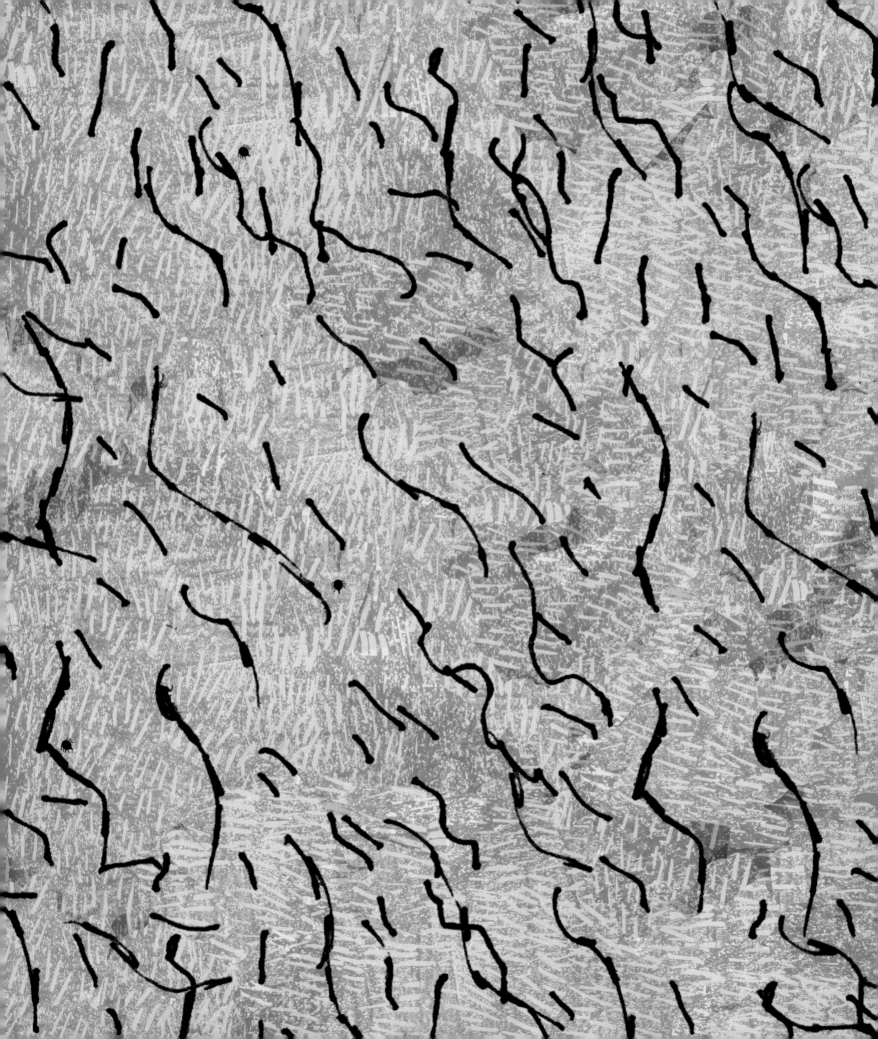